## NATIONAL GEOGRAPHIC

# MORE PLACES TO VISIT

## Nick Bruce

There are many famous places to visit in the United States.

Have you been to the **STATUE OF LIBERTY**? It is in New York City.

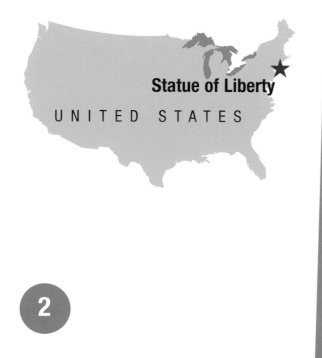

Statue of Liberty

UNITED STATES

The STATUE OF LIBERTY is one of the tallest statues ever built. It is a symbol of freedom. It is on Liberty Island in New York Harbor.

Have you been to the
**WASHINGTON
MONUMENT**?
It is in Washington, D.C.

**Washington Monument** ★

UNITED STATES

4

The WASHINGTON MONUMENT
is named after our first president,
George Washington.
It was built to help us remember him.

Have you been to the
GATEWAY ARCH?
It is in Saint Louis, Missouri.

Gateway Arch ★
UNITED STATES

The **GATEWAY ARCH** stands next to the Mississippi River. It's known as the gateway to the western half of the United States.

Have you been to the
GOLDEN GATE BRIDGE?
It is in San Francisco,
California.

**Golden Gate Bridge**

UNITED STATES

The GOLDEN GATE BRIDGE
is one of the largest suspension
bridges in the world.
The bridge hangs from cables
suspended between two towers.
The bridge connects San Francisco
to northern California.

Have you been to
**MOUNT RUSHMORE**?
It is in South Dakota.

★ **Mount Rushmore**

UNITED STATES

MOUNT RUSHMORE is a huge carving on a cliff. The faces of four presidents are carved into the cliff. They are George Washington, Thomas Jefferson, Theodore Roosevelt, and Abraham Lincoln.

Have you been to the
SPACE NEEDLE?
It is in Seattle,
Washington.

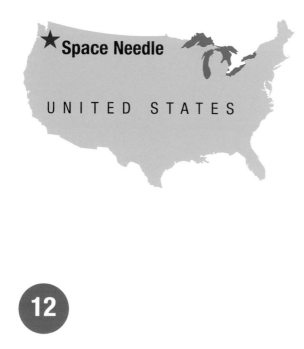

★ Space Needle

UNITED STATES

The **Space Needle** is an observation tower. It was built for the 1962 World's Fair.

# Have you been to these famous places?

Space Needle

Mount
Rushmore

Statue of Liberty

Golden Gate Bridge

Washington
Monument

Gateway Arch

# INDEX

| | |
|---|---|
| Gateway Arch | 6–7, 15 |
| Golden Gate Bridge | 8–9, 15 |
| Mount Rushmore | 10–11, 15 |
| New York City | 2 |
| Saint Louis, Missouri | 6 |
| San Francisco, California | 8 |
| Seattle, Washington | 12 |
| South Dakota | 10 |
| Space Needle | 12–13, 15 |
| Statue of Liberty | 2–3, 15 |
| Washington, D.C. | 4 |
| Washington Monument | 4–5, 15 |